MY MiniCamper
CONVERSION

A Fun Guide for the Conversion of a Minivan into a Minicamper
RV for under $150

CHARLES A MATHYS

Netcam Publishing
Naples, Florida

Published by Netcam Publishing

ISBN: 978-0-9843775-0-3

Dedication

For my wife, Marjorie.

As I write this dedication on our 54th wedding anniversary,
I realize that without my wife's support and understanding I would
not be able to spend all the time required to write books.

Acknowledgments

Many people helped me make this book possible. I sincerely thank, first of all, my wife, who let me tinker with the family car even though she is no longer interested in camping.

I also thank my friends Bob Spettle and Bob McKelvie for their many helpful suggestions and comments as they reviewed the manuscript.

My grand children were the ones who encouraged me to turn the plans into a book with their excitement about the project. With their parents, they were instrumental for refining the design as we tested the camper on many camping and boating trips. I received many good ideas for the title and the design of the cover.

My thanks also to my grandson Dan Robartes who designed and maintained our web-site since its inception. And, finally, a big thank you to Cheryl Sivewright/ Outsource-Design who designed a beautiful book cover with a few amateurish photographs taken in Key West.

Introduction

It would be a tall order to find a vehicle that can carry five adults in comfort, sleep two and carry all the gear for camping, picnics or tailgating parties. But, in fact, it can be done easily and inexpensively.

This book came about because I converted my new Toyota Sienna minivan into a mini camper. I put the plans on my web site "myminicamper.com". After installing a counter on the website, I noticed quite a bit of interest even though the web site was not promoted at all. The next step was to expand the plans shown on the web site to include a short history of the minivan and the specifications of the vehicles that would be most suitable for conversion to a camper.

Purchasing a used minivan is an excellent way to obtain the basic vehicle, but care must be taken not to get one that is too old as it would tend to be smaller. The generations of minivans are described in Part 2. I also added the plans and instructions to convert many minivans other than the present generation Sienna to a mini camper.

I realize that most campers already have camping equipment that they want to use such as their camp stove, and camping table and folding chairs. Some of these items that may not be space efficient, so a couple of variations for their storage are offered in the designs.

With a vehicle as versatile as the minivan, different folks will emphasize different uses. For some, it will be mostly for use as a full size second car and utility vehicle to transport cargo. For others it will include trips to the biking trails or the lakes or ocean for boating and fishing. Others will be mainly interested in traveling on a budget. And, surely, the younger generation will want to use the van for camping at music festivals and at camping sites.

All of these activities can be done in greater comfort with an RV. But in most cases, the RV is a far larger vehicle than the activity requires with the attendant higher operating costs as well as the cost of depreciation and insurance.

The book is divided in four parts:

- An overview of the minivan conversion
- The history of minivans and the current specifications of competing models
- The conversion of the Sienna minivan and the design of a number of camping accessories
- The conversion of other minivans that have adequate dimensions for camping

The total cost of the parts for the conversion of the Toyota Sienna is $132 as shown in the bill of materials. Anyone who can read a simple plan, take a measurement and handle simple tools is capable of doing an excellent job on this conversion in a weekend by following the simple directions.

Good luck finding a good minivan, and have fun using it as a minicamper!

Table of Contents

Introduction

1. Description and construction of the base; Appendix A

2. Description and construction of the partitions and the posts

3. Description and construction of the lid; the custom hinges; Appendix B

4. Description and construction of the organizer and the organizer cover

5. Description and construction of the folding table

6. Description of the paper towel dispenser and the lantern hook

7. Carpeting and underlayment.

8. Painting and Bill of Materials

1. Description and construction of the partitions and the posts

2. Description and construction of the Lid and Hinges

3. Fittting the Coolers in the Well

4. Camping Accessories

5. Bill of Materials and Final Thoughts

Appendix A: Full Size Base Patterns

Appendix B: Full Size Lid Patterns

Part 1.

OVERVIEW

of the

MINIVAN CONVERSION

Part 1.

Overview of the Minivan Conversion

The Minivan

RV's are great for camping and for the enjoyment of the great outdoors. But they are very expensive to buy and operate. The minivan is a great alternative: there is plenty of room for people and camping gear and the gas mileage is two or three times better than that of the large RV's. Moreover, it is much more practical as a second car.

As shown in the pictures below, bikes can be transported easily to the biking trails and a 10-foot kayak fits inside with room to spare. The sturdy roof rack can also be used to carry a large canoe or camping equipment. The average late model minivan has 10 cubic feet more room that a Chevrolet Suburban SUV.

For those who wish to own a simple inexpensive camper, the modifications described in the book transform the minivan into a great "minicamper RV". In addition to transporting bikes and kayaks, it provides sleeping accommodations for two at campgrounds or at music festivals. And, a full complement of camping gear makes it perfect for picnics and tailgate parties.

The Mini Camper RV Conversion

I bought the 8 passenger configuration of the Toyota Sienna because my plan was to remove the third row seats to make room for the sleeping area and the efficient storage of camping equipment. But, after these modifications were made, I still wanted to have a comfortable vehicle seating 5 adults for every day use as my second car.

The 8 passenger Sienna has the most usable space behind the second-row seats according to "Consumer's Report" with the Honda Odyssey and the Nissan Quest very close seconds. Other makes and model years of minivans can also be converted into excellent "minicamper RV's". The pros and cons of various new and used models are discussed in the book. The most important dimensions to be considered are the size of the well for the coolers and the storage of the camping gear and the distance to the rear of the second row seats for the sleeping area.

Sleeping Arrangements

The Sienna (and other minivans with similar dimensions), has 5 feet of flat space in back of the second row seats and 6 feet 4 inches when the second row seats are folded forward. By preserving this area while modifying the large well for storage, it was possible to provide a sleeping area the size of double bed (50 by 76 inches) as seen in the picture below.

I added a carpet with underlayment in addition to the standard carpeting and underlayment which comes with the van. These four layers of padding provide a firm but comfortable sleeping surface. However, for an older adult like me, a self-inflating camping pad provides much greater sleeping comfort. Two "Eddie Bauer" 2 ½ inch, self inflating mats, 25 x 76 inches, fit perfectly in this space.

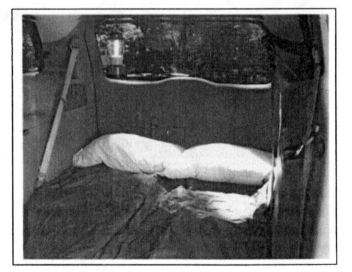

The coolers and the cover over the organizer have no padding but, since this is where the head rests, large, comfortable pillows provide adequate support.

Storage for food, Camping and Picnic Gear

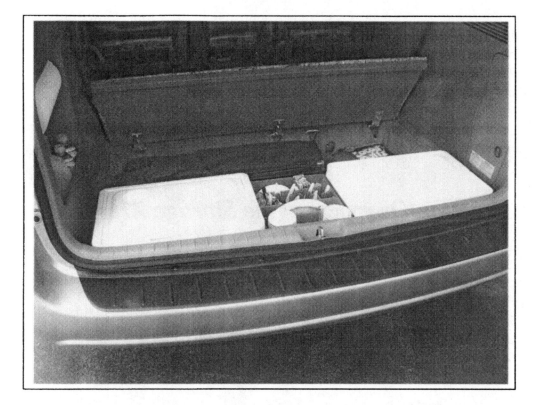

Normally, the third row seats fold into the rear well. By removing these seats and covering the top of the well with a plywood lid, a large amount of storage (8 cubic feet) is made available while 5 people can still sit comfortably in the van. As shown in the picture, two coolers with flat tops (26 quart size) fit perfectly into the back part of the well. One cooler functions as a refrigerator while the other is used to store baked and packaged goods.

The space between the two coolers is used to store and organize the plates, cups and utensils. This area can store the following: 25 10-oz hot cups and 40 8-oz cold cups, 25 10 inch paper plates, 25 3.5 inch paper bowls, and, at least 50 plastic forks, spoons and knives.

There is also room for the salt and pepper shakers and packaged condiments such as mustard and ketchup as well as other items such as lighters, openers and utility knives that are used often and must be kept handy. Below the organizer, there is additional space to store paper plates and bowls.

In front of the coolers and organizer, there is a deep, one by four foot storage area for camping and picnicking gear. In this space, the following can be stored: a two burner Coleman propane stove, a custom 22 inch by 24 inch folding table made according to the plans, 2 folding seats, pots and pans and an electric lantern. Canned and packaged goods can also be stored in this space.

Over this storage area, a hinged plywood cover provides the support needed for the sleeping area.

Construction Overview of the Storage Area

One of the goals of this project was to install the storage area framing and the lid over the well and attach them to the car without drilling holes or modifying the Sienna minivan in any way.

The back seats were removed by taking out the 4 bolts that attach the seat legs to the bottom of the well. By replacing these 4 bolts with longer ones, a 3/8 inch plywood base approximately one by four feet was secured to the bottom of the well to the anchor nuts that were used for the seats.

The partitions which separate the space in the well are attached to this base. They hold the coolers in place and support the lid and the utensil organizer. The partitions are cut from a 12 foot piece of 1 by 4 as shown in the picture. The lid is supported by four posts about 10 inches long

The lid is a piece of 3/8 inch plywood approximately one by four feet. It is attached to 3 of the 4 seat locks with custom hinges. These hinges squeeze the seat locks so that, when the lid is opened, it remains in that position. As the picture shows, the hinges are made of 2 pieces of 1/8 inch aluminum.

Detailed plans and full size patterns to cut the plywood as well as a bill of materials are provided in the book to expedite the construction job and minimize waste.

The plans also show the utensil organizer's construction: the sides are built of 3/8 inch plywood while the dividers are built of ¼ inch plywood. They are all glued together and to the sides. The exact configuration is, of course, the designer's choice.

Not shown is a 10 by 13 inch, 3/8 inch plywood cover over the utensil area which is attached to the back of the lid with two hinges to provide a head rest.

More Camping Goodies

In the storage area to the left of the well (as shown in the picture below), there is room for about 2 gallons of water in containers of various sizes. Above the water storage, a paper towel dispenser is installed. This is an item which is always very useful at picnics

A hook for the camping lantern was installed in the overhead seat belt storage area. The standard grocery bags hooks are used to hang rubbish bags or can be used to support a wide shelf

A folding camping table described in the plans (see the pictures above and below) was designed to fit in the storage area. In its open position it measures 22 by 24 inches. The 26 inch height is about right to match the height of the folding chairs. The stubs to which the legs attach are 4 inches long. They serve two purposes: the table legs attach to them and the 2 burner Coleman propane stove fits safely under the table in the storage area in front of the cooler while allowing heavier objects such as the folding chairs to be stored on top. (See the picture above).

There are many 12 volt devices that can plug into the 12 volt outlets above the paper towel dispenser and in the front console. I use three of these: an electric bicycle tire pump, a spot light and a two cup electric beverage heater which heats water for coffee, tea or soup.

Summing Up

So there you have it: a fully equipped minivan camper RV that sleeps two in comfort and can also be used for picnics or tailgate parties for about $132 including the coolers and the carpeting. If more room is needed for camping there are several types of tents and awnings that attach to the open liftgate.

The camping conversion was made without modification to the vehicle. The weight of the additional carpet, underlayment, coolers, partitioning, folding table and chairs, camp stove and the many accessories is about 75 pounds while the weight of the 2 seats that were removed is 94 pounds. The net weight is decreased by about 20 pounds, so there is no negative effect to the mileage which is very good: better than 25 mpg on a trip.

The users of this versatile, multi-purpose fun machine are many. For the younger set, their main interest might be attending music festivals. For energetic oldsters it might be to travel on a budget while stopping at campgrounds or motels.
For everyone, this mini-camper is an excellent second car, a roomy transporter of bikes and small water crafts and it is fully equipped for picnics, tailgating and camping. Whenever the great outdoors beckons, this mini-camper RV is ready for action.

Part 2.

SELECTING AN

APPROPRIATE

MINIVAN

Part 2

Selecting an Appropriate Minivan

Minivan History

The minivan that we are familiar with today originated in 1984 as a Plymouth Voyager from Chrysler Corp under the direction of Lee Iacocca. It was hardly the first van used to carry people and cargo: VW launched its "Microbus" decades earlier in 1950. It had a 25 HP engine and measured 186 inches long. It became the 60's and 70's generations beloved "Hippie Mobile".

Built on a "K" car platform, with its front wheel drive, low flat floor and a capacity of 125 cubic feet, the 1984 Plymouth was an instant success, selling 209,000 units in its first year. Since then millions of minivans have been produced by American and foreign manufacturers. The Chrysler/Dodge models on sale today are the company's 5th generation models. Interestingly, the new style is again boxy like the original Plymouths.

As the chart below shows, the eight main competitive models for 2009 all have very similar sizes and weights. Note that the Chrysler, Dodge and VW Routan are built on the same platform and so are the Hyundai Entourage 4 door and the Kia Sedona LX and EX.

Minivan Name	Wheelbase	Length	Volume	Weight
Chrysler/Dodge/VW	121.2 in	202.5 in	143.8 cu.ft.	4335 lbs
Toyota Sienna	119.3 in	201.0 in	148.9 cu.ft.	4270 lbs
Honda Odyssey	118.1 in	202.1 in	147.4 cu.ft.	4387 lbs
Hyundai/ Kia Sedona	118.9 in	202.0 in	141.5 cu.ft	4387 lbs
Nissan Quest	124.0 in	204.1 in	148.1 cu.ft	4293 lbs

What Does the Chart Tells Us?

The chart tells us that all 2009 minivans are large vehicles, much bigger than they appear, weighing about 4300 lbs on average with an average of about 146 cubic feet of cargo space.

To put those numbers into perspective: it takes a car as large as the $60,000 Lexus LS 460 which also weighs 4300 lbs and measures 198 inches in length to match the size of an average minivan.

Compared to an SUV, it takes the behemoth of the American road namely the Chevy Suburban to match the minivan. The lightest two wheel drive Suburban weighs 5600 lbs, it is about 20 inches longer than the average minivan yet it has a cargo space of 137 cubic feet (10 cubic feet less than the minivans).

Quoting from "Consumer's Guide", it is not an exaggeration to say that the minivan is: "Easily the smartest use of space and cargo. Best blend of comfort, convenience and safety features"

7 and 8 Passenger Models

Of the 2009 models only Toyota and Honda offer an 8 passenger minivan. Since the 3rd row seats will be removed to make room for the camping gear and the sleeping accommodations, the seating configuration is important to consider in any new or used car buying decision.

Over the last 25 years, a number of 8 passenger minivans have been produced. My daughter had Pontiac Montana (Chevrolet had a similar model) with 2 bench passenger seats. She tells me that the rear well was too shallow for camping gear and coolers.

I should point out that there are advantages to some of the 7 passenger configurations. The path between the two second row seats is a convenient passage to the back of the van. That space can also be used to fit the front wheels of two bikes without the need to fold one of the three seats in the eight passenger configuration of the Sienna. In the Chrysler models the two second row seats fold into the floor. This feature clears an eight foot area (the proverbial 4 x 8 foot sheet of plywood area) for storage and sleeping.

Selecting a Used Model

Unless you presently own a van that is appropriate for a conversion you may also be looking at used models. It is useful to know the model years of the various generations of vans that each manufacturer produced. You can expect that the basic specifications of each model year will not change appreciably during the entire generation's production cycle.

The chart below shows the model years of each generation of minivans produced in the last 25 years.

Minivan Type	1st Gen	2nd Gen	3rd Gen	4th Gen	5th Gen
Chrysler/Dodge/VW	1984-1990	1991-1995	1996-2000	2001-2007	2008-Pres
Toyota Sienna	1998-2003	2004-2010			
Honda Odyssey	1995-1998	1999-2004	2005-2010		
Kia/Huyndai	2002-2005	2006-2009			
Nissan/Quest	1993-1998	1999-2002	2004-2010		
Chevy/Pontiac	1990-1996	1997-2005	2005-2008	Uplander	
Ford	1997-2004	2004-2007	Ford Flex		

What Does the Chart Tells US?

A total of 22 generations of minivans are listed. On average, each generation was produced for about 5 years. As a general rule, each new generation becomes larger, heavier and more powerful than the preceding one. In the present generation of minivans, all have 6 cylinder engines with displacements ranging from 3.5 to 4.0 liters and an average of 236 HP. Fortunately, the gas mileage has stayed about the same over this time period.

Both Ford and Chevy have dropped the "Minivan" name and in favor of "Crossover SUV's" for their new entries. The Ford Flex has distinctive non-minivan styling such as swinging doors instead of sliding doors. Neither the Ford Flex nor the Chevy Uplander has characteristics suitable for a camper conversion. The Ford has an interior volume of only 84 cu. ft. and lacks a flat floor. The Chevy has no well because that's where the spare tire is stored.

Not all the brands have been as popular as the Chrysler/Dodge which sold 332,000 units in 2006. At the bottom of the list, we find the VW which only sold 3387 units and the Hyundai which sold 8400 in 2008. The Kia and Nissan did a little better selling 27,000 and 29,000 units respectively in 2008. Nevertheless, several million minivans are still on the road since the first Plymouth Voyager was built.

Two Important Characteristics

The two main attributes that we need for the camper conversion are room for sleeping accommodations behind the second seat and a deep well for cargo. In general, the early generations vans were smaller. It is, therefore, unlikely that you will find a deep well in an old van. The well size and the sleeping area of the current models are shown below.

Minivan (Last Generation)	Length x Width	Depth To Floor	Depth To Edge	Distance to Front Seat
Chrysler/Dodge/VW	2x4 feet	9.5 in.	11 in.	96 in.
Chrysler/Dodge (Pre-2008)	2x4 feet	9.5 in.	12 in.	96 in.
Toyota Sienna	2x4 feet	10 in.	12 in.	76 in.
Honda Odyssey	2x4 feet	10 in.	12 in.	74 in.
Kia and Hyundai	2x4 feet	10.5 in.	12 in.	74 in.
Nissan Quest	20 in. x 4 feet	9 in	12 in.	96 in.

What Does the Chart Tell Us?

The chart above shows the well size, the depth of the well from the bottom to the floor level and from the bottom of the well to the edge of the liftgate base (where the lock is located). It also shows the room available for sleeping when the second row seats are stowed forward or under the floor (Chrysler models). Only the current generation of vans (up to 2009) is considered in the chart except for the Chrysler group where the last 2 generations of minivans were measured. Except for the Nissan Quest which needs less room to store the third row bench seat, the wells all measure 2 feet by 4 feet.

The depth of the well to the floor level ranges from 9 to 10.5 inches. Obviously, the deeper wells accommodate the coolers more neatly but all minivans listed here have acceptable depths.

I would highly recommend purchasing a 26 quart "Picnic Basket" "Igloo" cooler and checking for fit in the well, especially if an older minivan is being considered. These recommended coolers are 11 ½ high. The edge of the liftgate base is 12 inches from the bottom of the well except for the newest generation of Chryslers which measures 11 inches. As we can see from several pictures in the "Overview" Part 1, this depth will provide a very acceptable gradual incline from the level of the minivan floor to the level of the cooler cover.

The Minivan that I Bought

Selecting a new or used minivan depends on personal preference, looks, familiarity with the brand, dealer service and availability. Fortunately, there is plenty of choice whether you are buying new or used. There is no need to buy something that does not fit your lifestyle just because the specifications are slightly different from the ideal measurements.

I bought the 2008 LE Sienna 8 passenger minivan (8 passenger vans costs $150 more than 7 passenger vans) and traded in a Mercury Sable station wagon. My reasons for buying the Toyota as opposed to the very similar Honda were the "Consumer's Report" endorsement, the good safety marks and the availability of a Silver Shadow Pearl unit (another name for white) at a nearby dealership.

The sticker price was $28,174 including the LE, EVP package and the cost of delivery. The Toyota "extra value pack MRSP discount" brought the sticker price down to $27,189. The $1500 rebate program and the dealer discount of $2189 brought the price down to $23,500.

Negotiating that price was the easy part. Getting the full value for my trade-in according to the "Kelley Blue Book" ($8700) was much more difficult. But as they say, "the customer is always right", so I eventually won.

I am very pleased with my first Toyota. It is quiet, reliable and the performance is very good. The camper conversion is used routinely, mostly for picnics. It is equally useful for transporting bikes and the kayak and doing some camping.

The mileage on the sticker: 17 city, 23 highway is significantly understated. My last trip to Florida from Massachusetts via Washington DC and Raleigh NC was just over 1600 miles: 1500 highway and 100 city. The overall mileage was 27.8 mpg. I am not a fast driver but I move along with the traffic without exceeding the speed limit which is 70 in the Southern states. I like the gear ratio which allows the engine to run at a low 2000 rpm at a highway speed of 70 mph. I do inflate the tires to their maximum limit of 35 psi cold using an accurate dial gauge. This action alone probably increases the mileage beyond the highway rating.

As I mentioned in the overview, every effort was made to convert the minivan without modification to the vehicle or even drilling holes if it could possibly be avoided. In my experience, at trade-in time, the dealer wants to see a stock vehicle without extra parts. It should be possible to remove the conversion parts in less than an hour and replace the third row seats with the originals still in pristine condition.

Review of the Information Above

- All competitive minivans have very similar sizes and power plants

- The 2009 models range from second to fifth generation models

- Used models of older generations tend to be smaller

- 7 or 8 passenger configurations are available mainly in newer models

What comes next?

The next two parts of the book are the detailed designs, plans, instructions, and bills of materials for camper conversions and camping accessories. Part 3 describes the conversion of my late model Toyota Sienna. It applies, therefore, to all second generation Sienna models from 2004 to 2010. Part 4 a "generic" set of plans based on the design shown in part 1. It applies to all other minivans. The dimensions shown in the plans for different models of minivans will not be as accurate as for the Sienna because I only built one conversion kit for two popular minivans: a 2006 Chrysler/Dodge and 2005 Honda Odyssey. Bills of materials are included for each conversion.

Part 3.

THE 2008 SIENNA

MINIVAN CONVERSION

Part 3.

The Sienna Minivan Conversion

1. Description and Construction of the Base

As we will see, a major difference between the present generation of Siennas and most other minivans is the way the third row seats are attached to the body of the van. The Hyundai and the Kia Sedona EX come closest to the Sienna configuration. Consequently, the main difference between this and the generic installation is the way the partitions and the lid hinges are installed.

In the Sienna, a plywood base is used to support the partitions and the lid is hinged to the seat anchors with a custom designed hinge. In the generic design, the partitions are bolted to the bottom of the well and stock cabinet hinges are used. The partitions are used to support the posts and the organizer and keep the cargo in place when the coolers are removed for cleaning.

The base consists of a piece of 3/8 inch plywood measuring 41 ½ inches wide in front and 46 ½ inches wide in back. The front and the back of the base are straight lines. The full size patterns in Appendix A show the shape of the sides.

To put the two patterns together, cut along the line indicated on the second page and attach it to the first page with transparent tape. The height of the pattern should measure 11 ¼ inches. Then, cut along the center line of the pattern to provide a guide for the left (driver's side) and right side of the base. Cut the patterns on the outside of the heavy lines and trace the shape of the two side edges onto the plywood. Use a saber saw or a coping saw to cut the plywood.

Since the base is 11 ¼ inches deep (front to back) and the lid is 12 ¾ inches deep, these two pieces of plywood can be cut out from a 2 by 4 foot piece of 3/8 inch plywood which is available at "Home Depot" and other lumber yards.

The third row seats of the Sienna are attached to the bottom of the well using four metric bolts 8 x 1.25-20 mm long. By replacing these bolts with four bolts 8 x 1.25-40 mm long and using four 3/8 flat washers, the base can be attached securely to the bottom of the well without modification to the vehicle.

The drawing shown on the next page: "Base, Partitions and Posts" indicates the approximate location of the bolt holes. They are located 4 inches from the front of the base at distances varying from 2 1/8 inches to 17 3/8 inches from the center line of the base. These measurements need to be double checked in the vehicle before drilling the four 3/8 inch holes in the plywood base.

Temporarily attach the base so that the partitions can be positioned on the base and marked. Hint: be sure to line up the base holes with the anchor nuts in the well with a Phillips screwdriver that is held in a vertical position. This will avoid cross-threading the bolt into the nut. After the first bolt is loosely tightened, check the other three bolt locations again with the Phillips screwdriver. Widen the holes slightly if necessary.

Do not over-tighten the bolts to the point of distorting the shape of the plywood. But after a day or two, the carpet and the underlayment will compress and a few more turns can be taken up on these bolts.

As with all the wood in this project, the edges should be sanded and the corners should be rounded. Use 100 grit sandpaper to do this job by hand.

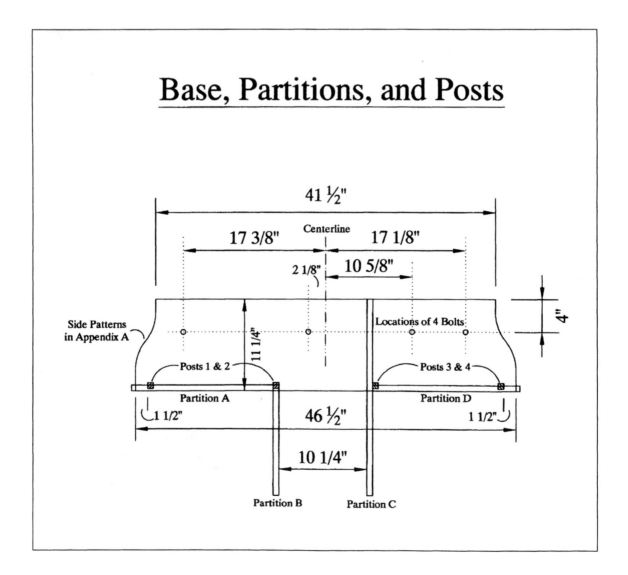

Base, Partitions, and Posts

2. Description and Construction of the Partitions and the Posts

The picture below shows the location of the partitions and the posts as they are attached to the base. On the following page you will find a drawing showing the dimensions of the partitions and of the posts.

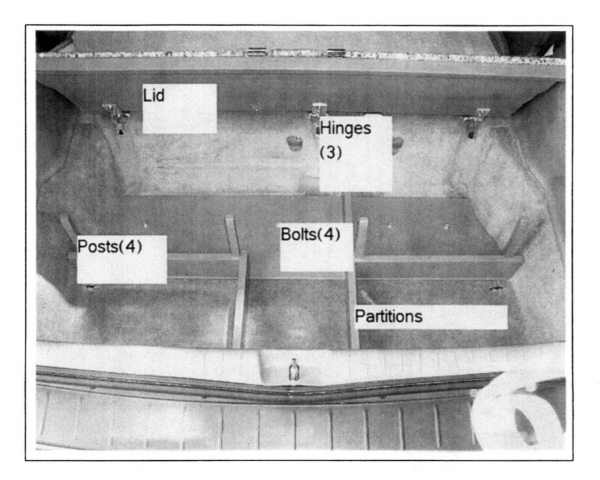

The four partitions and four posts are cut from a piece of 1 x 4 (3 ½ inches wide), 12 feet long. Cut off 4 ½ feet first and save this piece for the lid support and the 4 posts. Out of the remaining 7 ½ feet, cut out the four partitions according to the drawing on the next page. Note that partitions A and D are identical. Hint: it should be possible to use #2 pine (which is much less expensive than #1 pine) while avoiding the knots since the partitions and posts are short lengths of wood.

The slight angle at one end of the partitions will give the partitions a better fit to match the shape of the walls of the well which have a slight angle. The end of partitions B and C have to be rounded off for a better fit at the rear of the well.

Before gluing the partition pieces together and to the base, check for fit in the well by assembling the parts dry. 1 ¼ inch drywall screws can be used to secure the partitions to the base. Use 2 ¼ inch drywall screws to secure the partitions to each other.

Cut the 4 posts from the 4 ½ foot piece of 1 x 4 that was set aside, but first, rip a 1 inch strip of wood which is used to reinforce the edge of the lid. This 1 x ¾ strip should be free of knots.

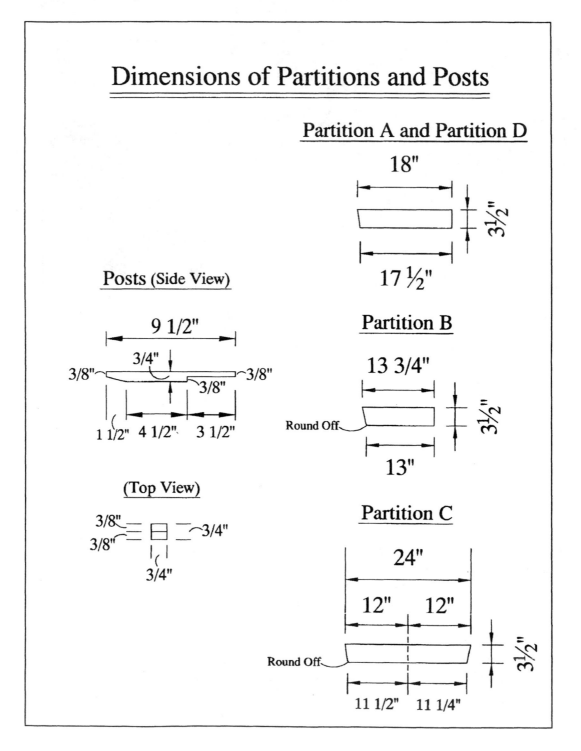

The posts have two functions: 1) to keep the coolers in place and 2) to support the lid. They are shaped as shown on the drawing above and are attached to partitions A an D as shown on the base drawing. The 1 ½ inch bevel is to facilitate taking the coolers in and out of the well. The 3 1/2 inch cuts provide greater support and save a little space when the posts are attached to the partitions with 1 inch dry wall screws. Hint: 1 ¼ inch drywall screws can easily be ground down to 1 inch.

3. *Description and Construction of the Lid*

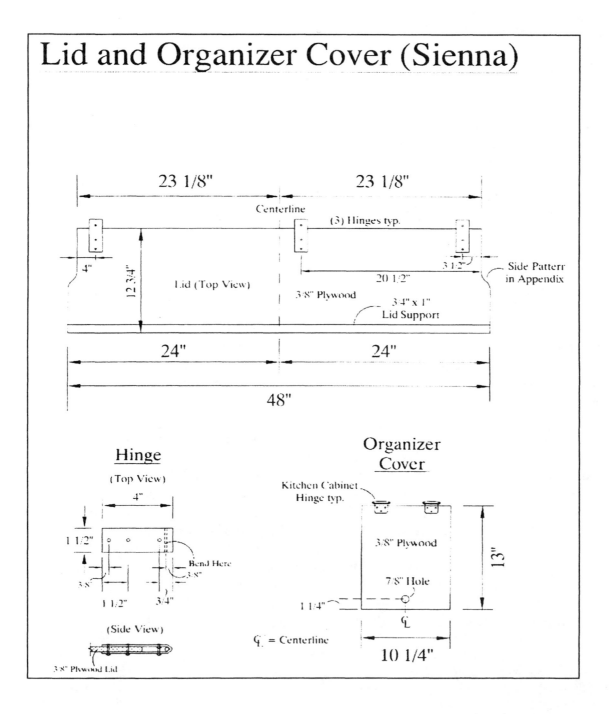

Lid and Organizer Cover (Sienna)

The lid covers the storage area in front of the coolers. It needs to be strong enough to support the weight of a person. The cover for the organizer area is attached to the lid. The lid shown in the drawing above is a piece of 3/8 inch plywood 46 ¼ inches wide in front and 48 inches wide in back. The front and the back are straight lines. The depth of the lid is 12 ¾ inches.

The shape of the sides of the lid is shown in the full size pattern in Appendix B. As with the full size pattern used for the sides of the base, the two pages are taped together after the second page is cut at the mark. The pattern is then cut out on the outside of the heavy line. Then, the assembled pages are cut in the middle to yield a left (driver's side) and a right side pattern with which to cut out the two edges of the plywood. The depth of the pattern should measure 12 ¾ inches. If desired, ½ inch plywood can be used for greater strength.

After the edges have been scribed and cut, attach the 1 x ¾ inch reinforcing strip of wood to the back part of the lid. This strip of wood can be attached in one of two ways: one way will lift the lid ¾ of an inch above the top of the posts, the other way will lift the lid 1 inch above the posts. Use five 1 ¼ inch drywall screws to attach the strip to the lid. After the hinges are assembled and it has been determined which way to attach the reinforcing strip in order to bring the lid even with the top of the coolers, the reinforcing strip can be glued and screwed to the lid.

The hinges are shown in the drawing on the previous page. They consist of 6 pieces of aluminum bar 4 inches long and 1 ½ inches wide. One end of each bar is bent over, starting at 3/8 inch from the end. This bending can easily be done in a large vise. Three holes are drilled in each bar to accommodate three 10-24, ¾ in long machine screws. Two machine screws are attached to the plywood while the third screw squeezes the 3/8 inch seat anchor. Note that this screw has a nut attached at the top of the aluminum bar. The reason for this nut location is to stop the hinge from moving forward.

Before drilling the holes in the plywood, attach the three hinges to the seat anchors and slide the lid between the two sections of the hinge. Adjust the location of the lid sideways so that it is centered and back and forth so that the 1x 3/4 reinforcing board rests on the top of the posts. When everything is positioned properly drill the plywood and install the remaining six 10-24 screws and nuts. Use a locking type of nut: a total of 9 machine screws and 12 nylon locking nuts are needed.

The organizer cover measures 10 ¼ by 13 inches and is cut from a piece of 3/8 inch plywood as shown on the previous drawing. It is attached to the center of the lid with two inexpensive kitchen cabinet hinges with a 3/8 inch offset. The 7/8 in. finger hole drilled in the cover is used to lift the cover easily.

4. Description and Construction of the Organizer

The organizer is used to store the cups, plates, knives, forks and spoons, 3 ½ inch bowls and the packaged condiments. The picture below shows the organizer neatly nestled between the coolers.

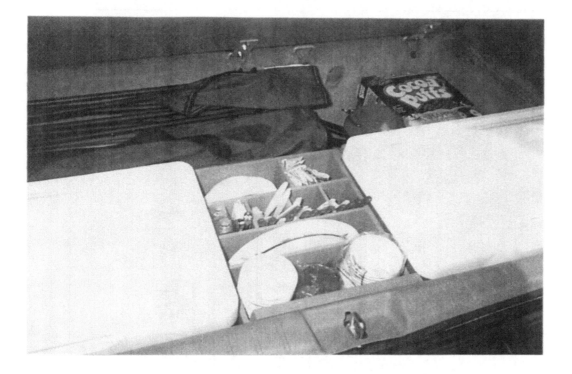

The organizer is constructed from 3/8 inch and ¼ inch plywood and one piece of ¾ inch plywood. This ¾ inch plywood can be made from two pieces of 3/8-inch plywood 10 ¼ by 11 inches glued together. It is used for two purposes: to hold the 3/8 inch plywood sides in place and to support the organizer cover.

As shown on the drawing on the next page, the ¾ inch plywood is set at a slight angle to conform to the shape of the well. It is 10 ¼ inches wide in order to slide between partitions B and C. The sides of the organizer attach to the ¾ inch plywood and rest on top of partitions B and C when installed. The overall size of the organizer is 13 ¾ inches by 11 ¼ inches.

Note that the first two sections of the organizer (from the rear to front) have no bottom so that as many cups as possible can be stored in the first section and so that 10-inch plates can be accommodated in the second section. There is a bottom to the next two sections to make these cubicles 5 ½ inches deep. A second bottom is added to the salt and pepper cubicle so that its depth is reduced to 3 inches for easier retrieval of the shakers.

There is a small amount of storage space under the second and third sections to store additional plates or bowls.

The 3/8 inch plywood sides and the ¼ inch parts are all glued together and attached to the ¾ inch plywood with two 1 ¼ inch drywall screws on each side. Hint: to hold the ¼ inch pieces in place while the glue dries, tiny ¾ inch brads can be nailed into the plywood.

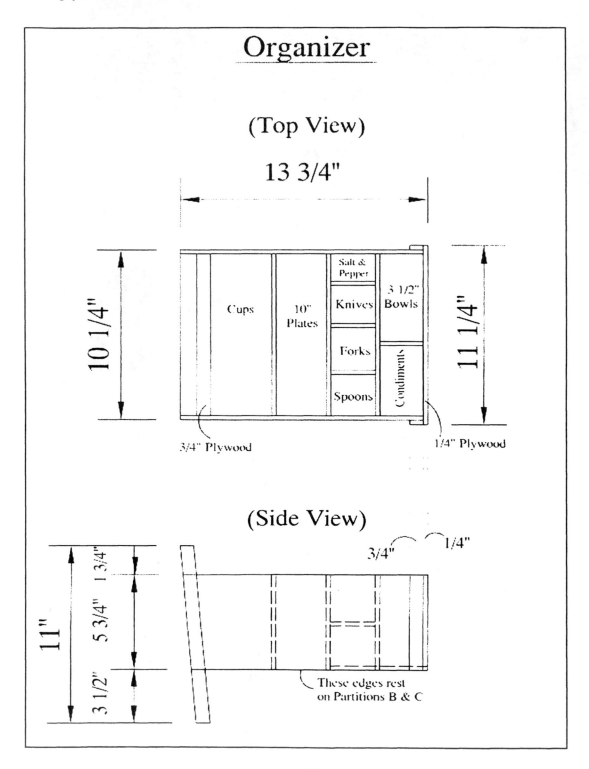

5. Description and Construction of the Folding Table

Although there are many folding tables on the market, I could not find one approximately 2 by 2 feet that was appropriate for the storage space in the front of the coolers. The one shown in the drawing below can easily be built out of 3/8 inch plywood. It measures 22 by 24 inches and just fits in the storage space.

A nice feature of this design is that the legs fit into leg stubs which are 4 inches long. When the legs are removed, the leg stubs hold the folded table 4 inches above the base. This provides a safe storage space for the camp stove underneath, while allowing heavier objects (such as the folding chairs) to be stored on top of the folded table.

It is, of course, up to the owner to select a camp stove, a table and chairs of his choice and to find a good way to store them in the available space.

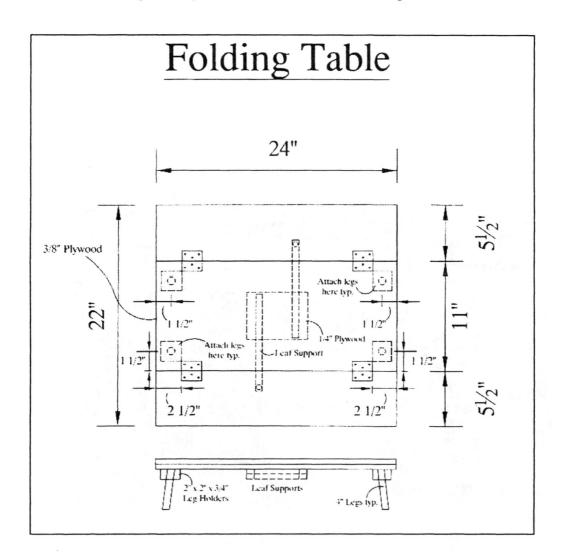

The table is built from a piece of 3/8 inch plywood. It measures 11 inches by 24 inches. The two leaves measure 5 ½ inches by 24 inches. The four hinges are located on the top of the table 2 ½ inches from the edge. The leg stubs are attached with 2 inch screws 1 ½ inches from the corners. A 5 to 10 degree angle adds to the stability of the table.
The stubs are glued in the stub holders which are 2 by 2 inch blocks of wood ¾-inch thick drilled to the size of the stubs. The blocks are located ½ inch from the sides of the table.

Although the hinges hold the leaves fairly straight it helps to add sliding leaf supports to the table. These can be constructed from 3/8 inch plywood. The sliding pieces are about 10 inches long and 2 inches wide. A 1 inch hole near the end provides an easy way to pull the slide from the slide holder.
The sliding pieces are held in place by a piece of 3/8 inch plywood approximately 6 by 7 inches separated by three pieces of 3/8 inch plywood measuring 1 by 6 inches.

The four legs can be built from a 10 foot piece of electrical conduit with an inside diameter of ¾ inches (or equivalent). The leg stubs are made from ¾ inch dowel material.
I found that legs measuring 25 inches provide about the right table height when the table is used with folding chairs.

6. *Description of the Paper Towel and Lantern Hook*

The storage cubicle at the rear of the minivan is large enough to hold about two gallons of beverages. Just above the containers there is room for paper towels which are always useful and should be kept handy. Just above the paper towels, there is a light and a 12 volt power outlet. On each side of the van there is also a grocery bag hook from which a plastic garbage bag can be hung.

A drawing of the paper towel holder is shown below. It consists of two 1 ½ by 2 inch blocks of wood ¾ inch thick. The blocks are cut on an angle so as to better match the sides of the storage cubicle. The holes and slots are 7/16 inch to accommodate a 3/8 inch dowel or a larger dowel turned down to 3/8 inch as shown on the drawing. The length of the dowel is 12 inches.

The blocks are mounted with 10-24 oval head screws so that the dowel hole is 15 ½ inches above the bottom of the storage cubicle.

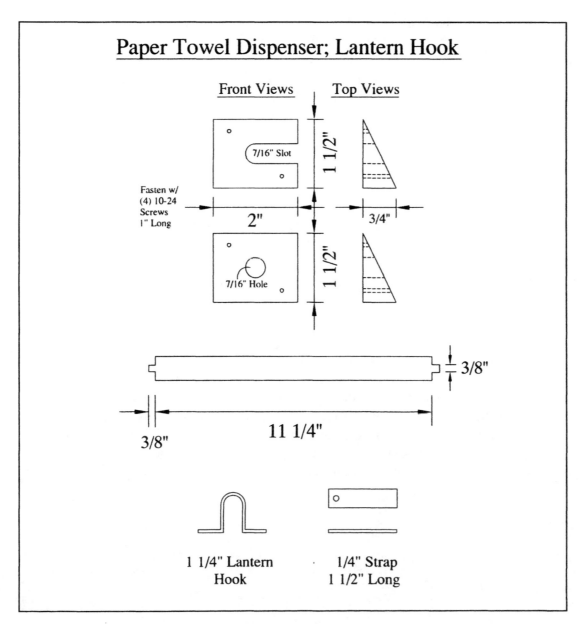

Paper Towel Dispenser; Lantern Hook

The 1 ¼ inch lantern hook can be bought at a marine supply store where in boating language it is called an "eye strap". There is just enough room in the recessed area of the middle seat belt to install the ¼ inch strap by 1 ½ inches long to hold the stored seat belt in place (without it, the seat belt keeps dropping out of the slots). Use 10-24 screws to install the lantern hook in the same area.

7. Carpeting and Underlayment

A remnant piece of carpet approximately 5 feet by 5 feet is needed to cover the rear of the minivan in back of the second row seats. The underlayment is a about one foot shorter because it does not cover the coolers or the organizer cover.

A paper or cardboard template is needed to cut the sides of the carpet and underlayment around the wheel well area. From top to bottom, the pattern should measure 59 ½ inches. Tape 6 sheets of 8 ½ in x 11in paper together and draw the contour of each side of the van on the paper. Cut out the excess paper and check your new template. Continue to make adjustments until the template fits within an eight of an inch of the sides of the van and of the wheel wells.

Turn the carpeting over and draw the outline on the back of the carpeting. Remember to use the driver side template on the right side of the carpeting seeing that it is turned over. Cut off the excess carpeting.

Repeat the procedure for the underlayment making it ¼ of an inch smaller than the carpet.

For a neat looking job, have the edges of the carpet bound at a carpet store.

8. Painting and Bill of Materials

I used a good grade of acrylic latex semi-gloss enamel from Home Depot. They matched the interior color of the van from the plastic panel which covers the car jack. I diluted the paint slightly with water to prime the surfaces and then put on a full strength second coat. One quart is just enough for the two coats. As previously mentioned all surfaces and edges have to be hand sanded before painting.

Bill of Materials

Two coolers: Igloo, 26 quart "Picnic Baskets"

3/8 in. plywood: 4 by 4 foot sheet or two 2 by 4 sheets

¼ in. plywood: 2 by 2 foot sheet

One 1 by 4 in. board, #2 pine, 12 feet long

Bolts: four metric 8 x 1.25, 40 mm long; 3/8 inch flat washers

1/8 in. aluminum bar 1/ 1/2 in. wide, 2 feet long (for the custom hinges)

1 ¼ in. and 2 ¼ in. drywall screws (2 dozen)

¾ in. (inside diameter) tubing (for the table legs), 10 feet long

¾ in. dowel material (for the leg stubs)

Hinges for the table: 2 by 1 ½ inches, brass, with 3/8 in. screws

Hinges for the organizer cover: kitchen cabinet hinges with 3/8 in. offset.

Four 1 in. pan head screws (for the front end of the hinge)

Six 8-24 x 1 in. oval head machine screws with nylon locking nuts (to attach the hinges to the organizer cover)

Eye strap, six 10-24 x 1 ¼ in. pan head screws (to attach the eye strap and the paper towel dispenser)

One quart of paint

The total cost of the materials listed above (purchased mostly at Home Depot) is about $132, including $35 for the two coolers (which I found at Target) and $30 for the carpeting.

.

PART 4.

THE GENERIC MINIVAN

CONVERSION

Part 4.

The Generic Minivan Conversion

In general, the generic conversion differs from the Sienna conversion in that the dimensions do not apply to a single model of minivan but rather they apply to all late model vans with appropriate well sizes of 2 x 4 feet and well depths of 9 inches or more.

The partitioning of the well is slightly different. In the Sienna conversion partition C (right side of the organizer) is shown going from front to rear across the cargo space of the well. The main reason is to keep the equipment separated from the food which can be stored in the smaller area. It is also necessary to keep the smaller pieces of cargo from sliding into the cooler areas when the coolers are removed for cleaning or to empty the ice water.

It is important to be able to store the large pieces of camping equipment namely, the camping stove, the folding table, the folding chairs and possibly a tent as compactly as possible. If it works out better to use the generic design shown here, that's fine. If the long partition C shown in the Sienna design is more appropriate to keep the cargo in place, it can be used instead.

1. Description and Construction of the Partitions and Posts

The drawing on the next page shows the location and the dimensions of the partitions with the short partition C. The partitions with posts attached to them hold the coolers in place, tightly enough so that they won't rattle but not so tightly that they can't be removed readily.

The dimensions shown for the four partitions, 13 ½ inches and 18 inches, are not exact due to slight variations in the well size of different vehicles. Trim these as necessary to have a tight fit around the coolers.

The height of the post is shown as 9 ½ inches which added to the thickness of the lid support and the 3/8 inch plywood lid and the underlayment totals about 11 ½ inches which is the same as the cooler height of 11 ½ inches.

The partitions, posts and lid support are cut from one of the two 1 x 4 by 8 foot # 2 pine board ¾ in thick. Since the pieces are short, it should not be difficult to avoid the knots that are found in the less expensive #2 pine.

As I described in the Sienna installation, the lid support (1 in x ¾ in) and the four posts can be cut out from one knot-free 4 foot piece of 1 x 4.

The partitions are glued and attached to each other with two 2 ¼ inch drywall screws. Note that partitions B and C extend beyond the end of partitions A and D by 3/8 of an inch. This makes them come out flush with the posts which are 3/8 inch thick at that point. It also avoids drilling holes for the screws near the corners.

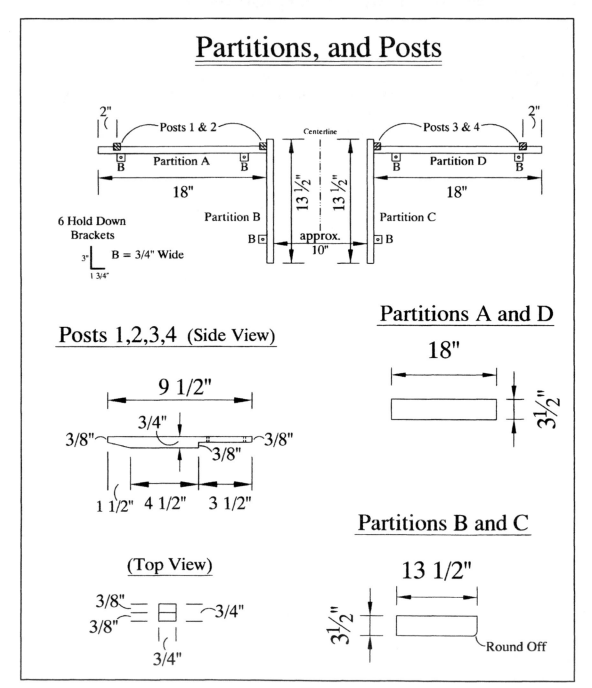

Unlike the Sienna installation where the partitions are attached to a plywood base, this installation requires 6 angle brackets that are attached to the bottom of the well. The drawing shows the brackets bolted to the well under the coolers. Actually, the brackets can be attached to either side of the partitions. The important thing is to have a clear area underneath the well. Make sure that when you drill the holes, there are no wires, tubes or supports in the way. Drill ¼ in holes to allow for a little "wiggle room" for the six 10-24, 3/4 inches long, flat head, stainless steel machine screws. Use nylon locking nuts with flat washers underneath the well.

At trade-in time, when the conversion is removed, ¼ inch plastic "locking hole plugs" (Home Depot and other hardware stores carry them) can be used to fill the holes. Hint: if you need a little more "wiggle room" the hole can be enlarged to 5/16 inch (5/16 inch and larger hole plugs are also available). Note that the 3 inch brackets were sawed off at 1 ¾ inches at the bottom so that only one hole has to be drilled in the well for each bracket. The bottom of the brackets are located flush with the bottom of the partitions and are held on the partitions with a total of twelve ¾ in flat head screws supplied with the brackets.

Mark the location of the 6 holes carefully so that the partitions will hold the coolers tightly in place. Hint: drill and install the middle bracket first and check the fit of the partitions around the cooler. Adjust for a tighter or looser fit as needed when drilling the other two holes.

The space between the coolers should be approximately 10 inches wide. Just as in the Sienna installation, this is where the organizer fits.

There is no need to repeat all the details of the organizer construction here. They can be found in Part 3 under "Description and Construction of the Organizer". The important points are that the organizer is built of 3/8 inch and ¼ inch plywood except for the ¾ in. end piece which supports the organizer cover (described later in this section).

The width of the organizer is determined by the location of the coolers. It may differ slightly from the 10 ¼ inch dimension shown, which, in turn will affect the size of the cubicles slightly.

The length of the organizer is 13 ¾ inches. It slides between the coolers and is supported by partitions B and C. It butts tightly against the back wall of the well.

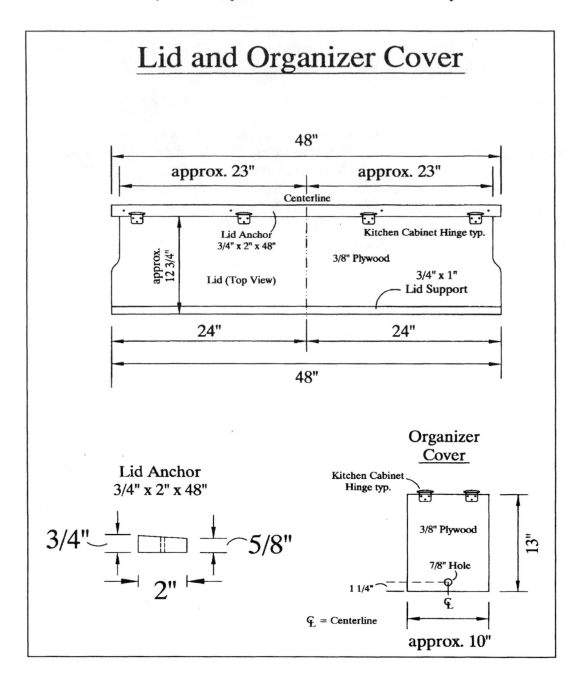

2. Description and Construction of the Lid

The lid covers the storage area and provides a solid base for the sleeping area. The lid shown in the drawing above is a piece of 3/8 inch plywood approximately 46 inches wide and 12 3/4 inches from front to back. Slight variations will occur depending upon the exact size of the well and the location of the lid anchor. ½ inch plywood can also be used for a stronger support but I have found the 3/8 inch plywood to be completely satisfactory.

The shape of the sides of the lid depends, of course, on the vehicle. A good place to start is to use the pattern shown in Appendix B. Follow the instructions to assemble the pages. Using the paper pattern make the necessary adjustments for a good fit. The 3/8 inch plywood can then be scribed and cut.

Next, the 1 x ¾ inch reinforcing strip can be attached to the back edge of the lid using five 1 ¼ inch drywall screws. At his point do not glue on the reinforcing strip to the plywood until it is determined whether the 1 inch or ¾ inch side is to be attached to the plywood. This will depend on the fit of the coolers at the bottom of the well. After the lid hinges are installed and the lid is properly secured, the screws can be removed and the strip can be glued and screwed in place.

In the Sienna installation, the seat locks which were used with custom hinges to attach the lid to the floor of the van were in a fortuitous location. In the generic installation, the anchor for the lid hinges has to be constructed from a piece of 1 x 4, ¾ inch thick as detailed below.

Rip a 2 inch strip 4 feet long from the second 8 foot piece of 1 x 4 #2 pine. The drawing shows that the thickness decreases from ¾ inch to 5/8 inch. This taper is to continue the slight incline of the lid from front to back. It will make it easier to fill the space between the anchor board and the floor of the van towards the front of the van but it is not vitally important.

Drill four ¼ inch holes: ideally two of them should be about 3 inches from the ends and the other two should be about 8 inches from the center line. Depending on the vehicle and the desired location just beyond the front wall of the well, it may be necessary to adjust these hole locations. The anchor board is attached to the vehicle with 4 pan head 10-24 stainless machine screws 1 ¼ inches long and nylon locking nuts. Flat washers are needed on top and on the bottom.

The hinges used in this installation are kitchen cabinet hinges with a 3/8 inch offset. They can be obtained at Home Depot or any good hardware store. Two of the hinges are located 4 inches from the edge of the lid and the other 2 are located 6 inches from the center line. The hinges are attached to the plywood with a total of 12, 8- 24 oval head machine screws ¾ inch long. Flat washers and nylon locking nuts are used on the back side of the plywood.

The hinges are attached to the ¾ inch anchor board with a total of eight, #8 ¾ inch long oval head screws. At this point of the assembly, the exact front to back dimension of the plywood can be determined and the lid can be trimmed as needed. With the coolers in place, the height of the lid can be adjusted by using the 3/4 inch or the 1 inch side of the reinforcing strip so that the lid comes up to the level of the cooler covers.

The last thing to be installed is the organizer cover. The same type of kitchen cabinet hinges with a 3/8 inch offset can be used. A total of 6, 8-24 oval head stainless machine screws ¾ inch long are needed with flat washers and nylon locking nuts. The organizer cover is centered and attached to the lid with four #8 oval head screws 1 inch long.

At this point the cover can be trimmed so that, from front to back, it rests fully on the ¾ end of the organizer and so that the sides just clear the coolers.

3. Fitting the Coolers in the Well

As we saw in the third chart shown in Part 2, all late model minivans except the Nissan, have 2 x 4 foot wells. However, due to the shape of the well or the configuration of the walls or the bottom, the coolers do not fit equally well in all vehicles. The photos below show how the storage area partitions and the coolers fit in the 2010 models of the Kia/Hyundai and Honda Odyssey and in the 2006 model of the Chrysler Town and Country.

The Kia/Huyndai Minivan

As shown above, the partitions built according to the measurements described in the plans fit perfectly in the Kia/Huyndai minivan.

On the next page is a photo of the two coolers as they fit within the partitions. Note that the height of the cooler tops is just below the level of the liftgate lock. The other important measurement is the space available for the organizer between the two coolers. In the Kia/Huyday it is 10 inches, just slightly less than the comparable distance in the well of the Toyota Sienna.

The Honda Odyssey

The picture below shows the fit of the two coolers within the partitions installed in a 2010 Honda Odyssey. The fit is not as good as in the Kia or the Sienna because the back part of the floor of the well is not as flat as the middle section. Consequently, the coolers tip slightly forward instead of hugging the rear wall of the well. A shim in the middle would fix the problem but it would necessarily lift the coolers just above the liftgate base. The distance between the coolers is 10 inches.

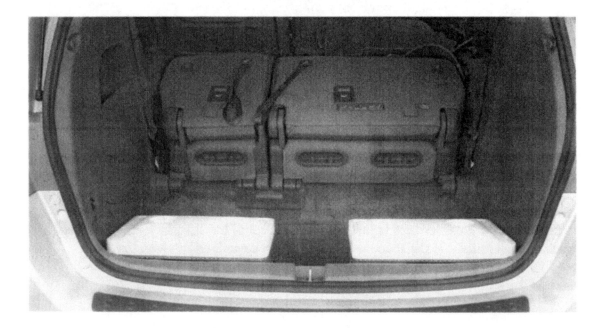

The Chrysler Town and Country

The photo shown below is of a 2006 Chrysler 2006 minivan. This is a 4th generation Chrysler/Dodge minivan. The main problem here is that the walls of the wheel wells interfere slightly with the sides of the coolers. Consequently, there is a 2.5 inch space on the side of the coolers. Although the well measures 2 by 4 feet, the distance between the tops of the coolers is only 5.5 inches.
Notice also, that the tops of the coolers are slightly higher than the lifgate lock due to the shallow depth of the well. I did not place the coolers in a 2010 model of the Chrysler minivan because the new design has an even lower liftgate base. Consequently, the results are likely to be less satisfactory.

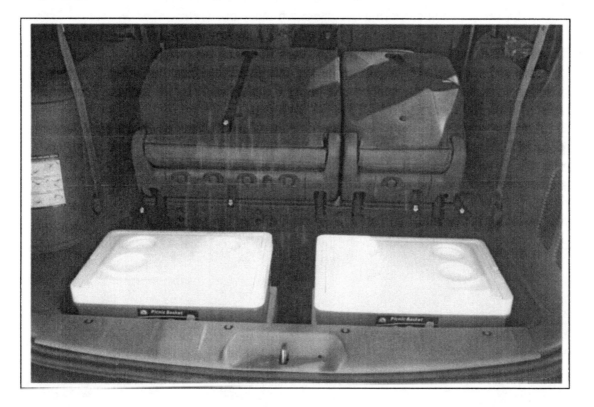

Conclusion

When selecting a minivan, whether new or used, to be converted into a camper, it is important to measure the size of the well carefully. An even better idea is purchase a cooler and to fit it into the well in its likely location. It will become immediately obvious if the well size is acceptable.
Considering only the use of the well area, I would rate the Sienna first, then the Kia, then the Honda, and finally the Chrysler/Dodge. As I mentioned before, the Chrysler/ Dodge minivans do have a superior feature for camping: the second row seats fold and disappear below the floor level leaving a flat 4 by 8 foot area to be used for sleeping.

4. Camping Accessories

Depending on your selection of camping gear, you may like to build the table described in Section 5 of the Sienna conversion.

Depending upon the vehicle being converted, you may also like to install a paper towel dispenser as described in Section 6.

The installation of the carpeting is very much the same as described in section 7. A slight variation is due to the addition of the lid anchor which sticks up above the floor by 5/8 of an inch. This gap can be filled in one of two ways.
1). Two strips of underlayment can be cut and glued together one being 3 inches wide by 48 inches and the second one being 6 inches wide by 48 inches. This double layer of underlayment should fill the 5/8 inch gap.
2) . Another way is to glue a 48 inch wide row of cedar shingles on a 1 by 4 foot piece of 1/8 inch plywood. The thick part of the shingle measures about 3/8 of an inch which will just about reach the top of the anchor board and provide the slight incline needed from the floor of the van.

The painting is described in Part 3, Section 8 of the Sienna conversion.

5. Bill of Materials and Final Thoughts

Two coolers: Igloo, 26 quart "Picnic Baskets"

3/8 inch plywood: 2 by 4 foot sheet,

¼ in. plywood: 2 by 2 foot sheet

Two 1 by 4 in. board, #2 pine, 8 feet long

1 ¼ in. and 2 ¼ in. drywall screws (two dozens)

Hinges for the lid and the organizer cover:
Six kitchen cabinet hinges with a 3/8 inch offset.

Eighteen 8-24 stainless machine screws, oval head, ¾ in. long, with nylon locknuts and washers. (For the lid and organizer cover)

Twelve # 8 stainless screws, oval head, ¾ in. long. (For the lid and organizer cover)

Four 10-24 stainless machine screws, pan head, ¾ in. long with nylon locknuts and washers. (For the ¾ inch lid anchor)

Six 10-24 stainless machine screws, flat head, ¾ in. long, with nylon locknuts and washers

Six 3 in. angle brackets ¾ in. wide with ¾ in. flat head screws (12 total) to attach to the partitions

Eye strap; two 8-24 pan head screws

One quart of paint

Optional:

¾ in (inside diameter) tubing (for the table legs), 10 feet long

¾ in dowel material (for the leg stubs)

Hinges for the table: 2 by 1 ½ inch, brass

The total cost of the above material (purchased mostly at Home Depot) is about $140, including $35 for the two coolers (which I found at Target) and $30 for the carpeting.

Final Thoughts

1. For me, the 5 passenger configuration of the minivan works out very well, but I can understand that many people need the 6, 7 or 8 passenger configurations during the work week preferably without having to remove all the camping gear stored in the well. It is possible to add a bench seat in front of the well without too much difficulty. The good news is that with approximately 32 inches from the front of the well to the back of the second row seat, there is plenty of room for a seat and reasonably good leg room. The other good news is that the seatbelts are already installed making the installation safe.

I have looked at dozens of seat installations in vans. The ideal would be a lightweight seat with an aluminum structure and a secure locking or latching mechanism that allows the easy removal of the entire unit.

The main challenge is to anchor the seat securely to the floor of the van while retaining the flat floor. I envision (without having built one) a 3 inch wide channel approximately ½ in height with captive nuts. It would replace the wooden anchor that was used to install the lid hinges in the generic configuration. The lid hinges would be attached towards the back of the channel and the seat anchors towards the front. A second such channel would be installed where the front of the seat frame is to be anchored. The Internet shows a number of "jump seats" and "bench seats" that may also be appropriate for such an installation.

2. When camping, a flat surface useable when standing is handy and a necessity for tailgate parties. I built a large shelf 17 by 52 inches which attaches to the hooks provided in the Sienna for the net used to secure groceries bags. As shown in the picture on the next page, the two sides are made of two 2 x 2's and the flat part of the shelf consist of four 1 x 4's. By having the edges of the shelf ¾ of an inch higher than the flat surface keeps the contents from sliding over the edge (this is always done in boats). The six parts of the shelf can easily be dismantled for storage and can be bundled into a compact 3 ½ x 5 x 52 inch package.

The four 1 x 4's are supported by two 1 x 2's 17 inches long (use the pressure treated wood which is stronger). They pivot on one end and have a slot at the other end which fits under the head of a #10 pan head screw. Be sure to get 1 x 4's and 2 x 2's that are straight and not twisted.

Each end of the 2 x 2's can be attached to the van in one of two ways. I chose to use the two existing grocery bag hooks and to add two more at the same height, about 16 inches forward. Barrel bolts or surface mount bolts (2 ½ inch size) as used on kitchen cabinet doors can also be used.

A good reason to use the grocery bag hooks is that they do not look like add-ons to the van. However, they cost $10 each and are not easy to install. To connect the 2 x 2's to the grocery hooks, I used 1/8 inch cotton cord (nylon is equally good) attached to the bottom of the 2 x 2's. A 2 inch loop beyond the end of the 2 x 2 works out well: the height of the top of the shelf is then 20 inches above the top of the coolers and 44 inches above the surface of the ground. As the picture shows the entire installation looks very neat.

3. The internet has numerous van accessories (Google: "Minivan Awnings") to add a tent or an awning to your minivan. The awning that I built as shown on the cover is simply a 6 x 9 foot painter's drop cloth. It is not waterproof but does a fine job providing shade and the materials cost less than $20.

The frame is made of 1 inch plastic pipe. The 2 poles in front are 2 x 2's but could be made of 1 ½ inch pipe as well. The 6 foot edges of the cloth were folded over and hemmed so that the pipe fits inside loosely (allow space for the 90 degree elbows). Two ten foot, one inch plastic pipes and two eight foot 2 x 2's (cut to about 76 inches) will do the job nicely.

4. We all know about some of the essentials for outdoor living and camping: bug spray, suntan lotion, and a first aid kit but some useful items not often thought of are a table cloth and a clothesline. When camping with a vehicle I would add: an extra camp light, a couple of flashlights and netting cloth to cover open widows. Framed screens custom made to fit the windows are, of course, better, but I found that the screen cloth attached with tape works very well.

God luck and enjoy the great outdoors!

About the

Author

Charles Mathys

Charlie Mathys was born in Brussels, Belgium and was brought to the US as a child but returned to Europe for his primary education.

At age 14, he returned to the US to stay. He learned to speak English while attending high school and by age 20, he had graduated from college obtaining a BS degree in electrical engineering from Northeastern University. In 1963, he acquired an MBA degree from Boston College.

After a 2 year stint in the US Army, he joined IBM at the very start of the computer era. He stayed at IBM for nearly 10 years before working for three small start-up companies doing computer research and development work hoping to find fame and fortune.

He finally settled down at Mitre Corp, a non-profit, "think tank" company doing consulting work for the Electronic Systems division of the US Air Force.
After retiring from Mitre, he combined his expertise in electronics and his love of boats to design an efficient electric motor for the propulsion of recreational boats. The results of his work were published in his first book "Electric Propulsion for Boats"

Several years later, he converted a minivan into a small camper. He refined and tested his design which is now being published in this book as a guide for the do-it-yourselfer who wants to enjoy the great outdoors with an inexpensive camper RV.

He lives in Massachusetts and Florida with his wife. From there, they often visit the families of their three children and seven grand-children.

Appendix A and B

Appendix A, pages 1 and 2 is used to cut the plywood base for the Sienna conversion. Appendix B pages 1 and 2 is used to cut the plywood lid. These four sheets are cut out as described as well as in the center. They are taped together with transparent tape at the marks to make up the templates needed to scribe the plywood.

Note that the patterns apply only to the Sienna minivan model years 2004 to 2010. For all other minivans, Appendix A is not used and adjustments will have to be made to Appendix B.

Appendices

The full size patterns needed to cut the 3/8 inch plywood base and lid are shown in the next 4 pages of appendix A and B. Cut and tape the pages together at AA and BB. Then cut them along the centerline to yield 4 patterns with which to scribe each end of the plywood. Separate the patterns to provide the overall dimension shown.

Appendix A: Plywood Base: Page 1

Overall Dimension

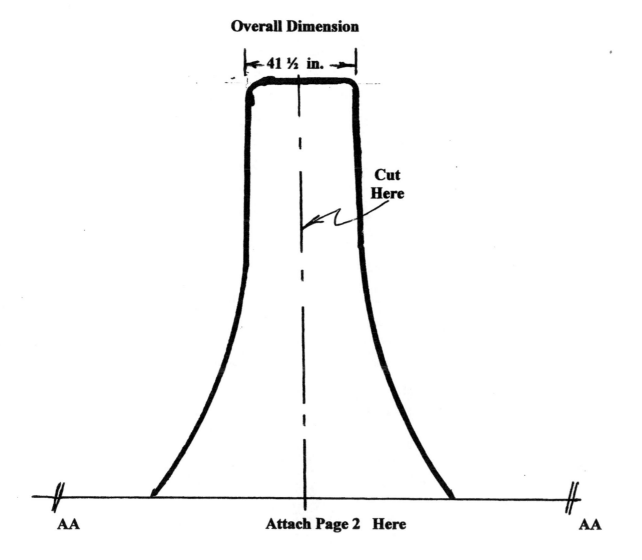

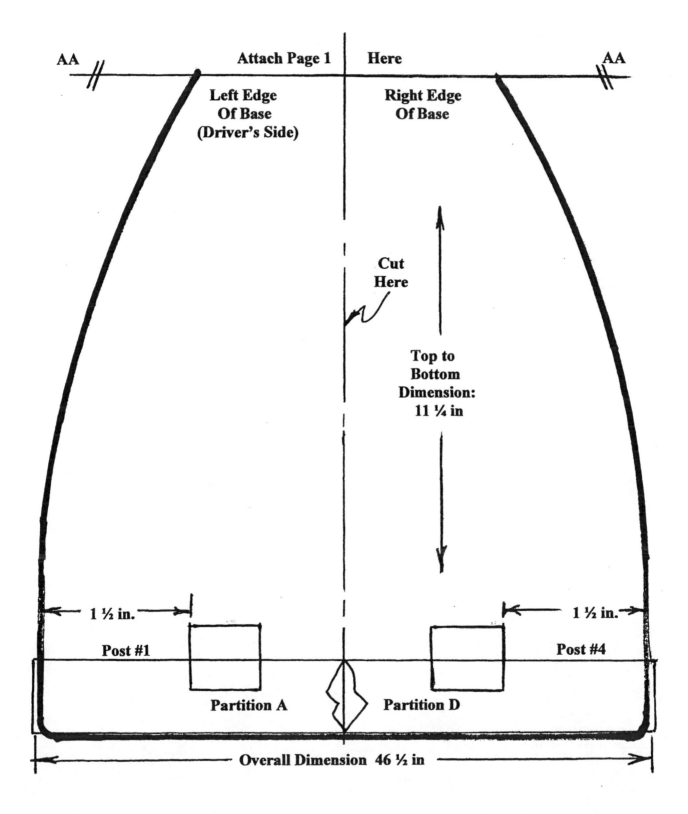

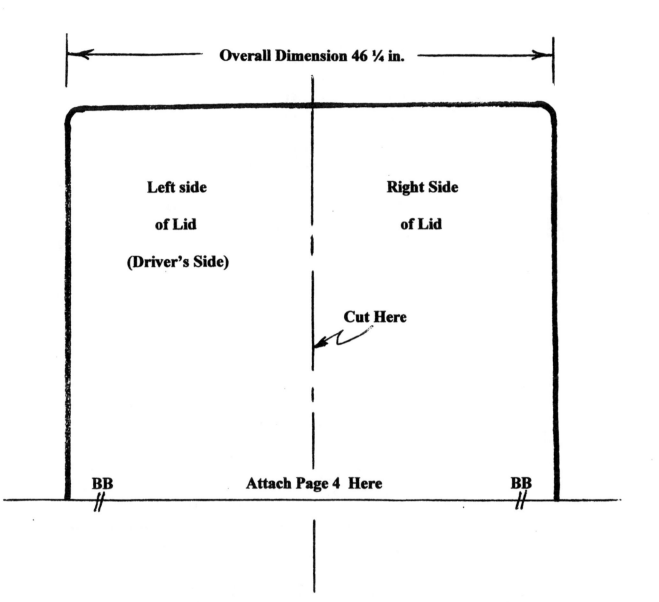

Overall Dimension 46 ¼ in.

Left side

of Lid

(Driver's Side)

Right Side

of Lid

Cut Here

BB

Attach Page 4 Here

BB

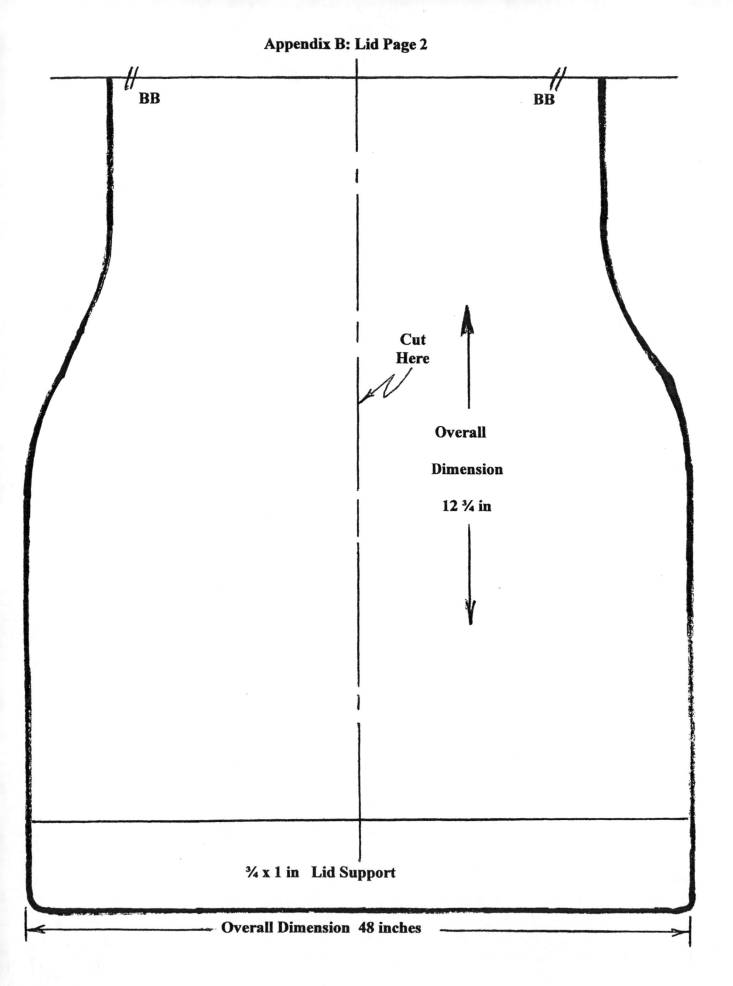

BB   **BB**

Cut
Here

Overall

Dimension

12 ¾ in

¾ x 1 in   Lid Support

Overall Dimension 48 inches

CPSIA information can be obtained at www.ICGtesting.com
Printed in the USA
LVOW09s1527050913

351164LV00003B/89/P